T0353738

Cherry Blossoms

LIESEL KIPPEN

Copyright © 2021 Liesel Kippen.

All rights reserved. No part of this book may be used or reproduced by any means, graphic, electronic, or mechanical, including photocopying, recording, taping or by any information storage retrieval system without the written permission of the author except in the case of brief quotations embodied in critical articles and reviews.

Balboa Press books may be ordered through booksellers or by contacting:

Balboa Press
A Division of Hay House
1663 Liberty Drive
Bloomington, IN 47403
www.balboapress.com.au
AU TFN: 1 800 844 925 (Toll Free inside Australia)
AU Local: 0283 107 086 (+61 2 8310 7086 from outside Australia)

Because of the dynamic nature of the Internet, any web addresses or links contained in this book may have changed since publication and may no longer be valid. The views expressed in this work are solely those of the author and do not necessarily reflect the views of the publisher, and the publisher hereby disclaims any responsibility for them.

Any people depicted in stock imagery provided by Getty Images are models, and such images are being used for illustrative purposes only.
Certain stock imagery © Getty Images.

ISBN: 978-1-5043-2428-1 (sc)
978-1-5043-2429-8 (e)

Print information available on the last page.

Balboa Press rev. date: 01/15/2021

BALBOA.PRESS
A DIVISION OF HAY HOUSE

Contents

1. The Forest at Night

By Liesel Kippen 🖤

Daylight closes her curtains

The whining dogs echo their moans.

Distraught screeches linger in the distance

Wolves howl intermittently, like mobile phones.

The full moon makes its stealthy appearance

Above the hauntingly quiet forest site.

All this unnerving harmonious commotion

Occurs significantly at the dead of night.

The forest at night is a lonely place
Towering, earthy trees dominate.
Sinewy, spiny, spindle-shaped branches
A setting for a scary movie, they create.
Outgrowths from their solid trunks
Stretch forth in all directions, rigid and tight.
They meander their sketchy, skeletal form
Towards a thin, dimly-lit band of grey light.

Darkness enshrouds this graveyard
Silhouettes dance around.
Movement is subtle and hesitant
Rustling leaves provide a solitary sound.
The wind gently blows the plumaged path
Of crackling undergrowth; nature's hearth.
The drowsy moon sheds silvery light
While hovered over the forest's looming height.

A fleeting shape covertly swaggers
As it tip-toes in the light.
It sends shivers up the spine
The heart immediately takes fright.
Perspiration beads form on the brow
Breathing erratically becomes the heart's plight.
The regular heartbeats are no longer in sync now
As the swaggering form takes flight.

A babbling stream in the background beyond
Quietly bubbles inconspicuously.
Deathly silence is no longer a threat
Consoling thoughts resume casually.
The soulful whine and distressed caterwaul
Have quietly eased for the night.
All the nocturnal sounds
House a moonlit symphony of sheer delight.

2. Lost between History's Pages

By Liesel Kippen 🩶

It's beautifully fascinating to get lost inside a History book
And navigate absorbingly through the relic's mystical, faded and rustic page.
Huddled up comfortably in a secluded spot in a minuscule nook
And tip-toe hesitantly into another setting, dimension, era and age.

The period of a powerful king's cruel and hostile reign
One of tyranny, unrest and an insatiable greed.
The land's people; victims of terror, wrath, fear and pain
Left desolate, poverty-stricken, hungry and in dire need.

Driven by ambition for wealth, fortune and fame
Pushed by a burning desire to acquire more.
All to secure and proclaim sovereignty and a name
For himself, from every land, territory and shore.

The final chapter, from cover to cover, once read
Of a tumultuous and prognostic era, leaves much unsaid.

3. An Owl's Prowl

By Liesel Kippen 🖤

The moon hung low in the darkened skies
Not a single sound could be heard.
Everything had become deathly still
Something out there was feared.

The ominous silence filled the air
Shadows were cast on the desolate plain.
The moon now shed a misty glare
This land had n't seen any rain.

Nothing moved, not even the grass
While perched on a branch sat an owl.
Its gaze pierced right through the dark
As its head tilted acutely on the prowl.

Its eyes focused and stared fixedly
At a subtle movement below.
Could it have been a defiant rat
That caused it to descend from the bough?

Its movements were deft and determined
While its vision a blurred blob and unclear.
Its sensitive whisker-like bristles
Signalled that a hearty meal was near.

With its large eyes fixed in its sockets
And its vision far-sighted and dim.
Its binocular vision sky-rockets
As it spins its entire head on a whim.

The owl gently glides its way through the air
A straight angle formed, by powerful wings of grey.
Its body gently and strategically aligns itself
To inaudible sounds from its unsuspecting prey.

It detects the difference in volume and time
And gracefully begins its downward flight.
The scuttling, scurrying, creeping, scampering
Is noted even at this very dead of night.

Gently flapping its outstretched wings
The owl begins its meandering plight.
It calculates precisely where the sound is from
As it traces the narrow strip of moonlight.

The owl makes its daunting downward spiral
And circles the ground's bird-eye views.
Then darts left, right, up and down
Adjusting its course as its prey moves.

The owl launches itself from mid air
And dives in for the swoop.
Then stealthily pounces on its victim
As it makes a loop in its scoop.

The rodent dangles lifelessly
In the owl's steely vice-like grip.
Grains of sand quietly descend
From the rodent's now frozen lip.

All resumes its corpse-like state
As the moon quietly saunters above.
Her shimmering pearly streaks of light
Hide pursuits not done in love.

4. Predator

By **Liesel Kippen** 🖤

Fiery eyes
Steel-like stare.
Sinewy thighs
Fixated glare.

Silent pants
Somber state.
Raucous rants
Nonchalant bait.

Evening blaze
Deadly plight.
Narrow gaze
Blackened night.

Grassy haze
Stiffened jaw.
Intense phase
Tensions raw.

Darting eye
Twitching ear.
Emotions high
Sudden fear.

Bristled brush
Pensive wait.
Adrenalin rush
Destined fate.

Graceful stance
Stifled growl.
Majestic prance
Hungry prowl.

Creased brow
Sunken head.
Contorted bough
Looms ahead.

Shrivelled branches
Dried up leaves.
Nature's nuances
Destiny cleaves.

Crimson sky
Desolate plain.
Scarlet eye
Shaggy mane.

Sudden romp
Oblivious game.
Frantic stomp
Devious mane.

Foreboding lunge
Pulsating vein.
Decapitating plunge
Languished frame.

Deathly quiet
Frozen air.
Inward riot
Bloody fare.

5. Life, though imperfect, can beautifully entice

By Liesel Kippen 🩶

The sun rises and her beauty shines through
Her golden rays spread randomly too.
Some days are dark and filled with gloom
Rainclouds huddle like relics in a tomb.
Morning embraces us with her glistening glow
Evening descends like a distant foe.
Moments are n't always wonderfully nice
Life, though imperfect, can beautifully entice.

Courage is a beautiful thing
It makes us laugh and it makes us sing.
Sometimes fear and doubt take hold
When life comes crashing and leaves us in the cold.
Joy gushes through like a broken tap
Sadness wakes stealthily from her nap.
Moments are n't always wonderfully nice
Life, though imperfect, can beautifully entice.

Tumultuous feelings rise to the fore
When disaster strikes our inner core.
Pain and sadness inwardly unite
They overwhelm with grief, collaborate and fight.
Love and romance rise in the hour
Filled with valour, strength and power.
Moments are n't always wonderfully nice
Life, though imperfect, can beautifully entice.

Hardships plague and grip like a vice
They stab, wound and pierce like a knife.
Failure dominates and depresses the soul
Leaving it vulnerable and caged in a hole.
Positive mindsets emerge from the blue
Empowered by confidence and resilience too.
Moments are n't always wonderfully nice
Life, though imperfect, can beautifully entice.

6. Pain

By Liesel Kippen 🖤

Feelings intense of mental torment
Its agony felt as the body lies spent.
Strips from the beating heart are rent
Fragile memories, twisted and bent.

A dull tormented semi-lifeless throb
Gnaws at, contorts the gutted blob.
Anguish, remorse, a superfluous sob
Sagging soul, exhausted, it robs.

Shredded feelings and emotions bare
Tattered, dissipated, without a care.
Intolerable levels of layers it tears
Scattered in its emotionally decomposing lairs.

Dispersed, dispelled, memories in disarray
Dislodged, dismantled, emotions in decay.
Detached, devoured thoughts fray
Deluded, deprived feelings stay.

Savagely wrenched, the heart's beat
Poignant, acute, now bittersweet.
Plunderous, pillaged, intolerable feat
Overpowering, excruciating, irremediable heat.

Pain shows no mercy, it debilitates
Then moves in defiantly and incapacitates.
Leaving its victims in disorientated states
To reorientate and excogitate.

7. Renewed Hope

By Liesel Kippen 🖤

The moment Lee had dreaded
Had now descended upon her.
Anguishing thoughts silently
And numbingly drowned her.

Guilt coursed through her soul
And pierced her like a needle.
Plunging its way downwards
Without any wheedle.

As tears welled up inside of her
And formed covertly in her eyes.
She looked upwards painfully
For an answer in the skies.

Lee had let her team down
By not supporting them on the day.
She had chosen rather to stay at home
And there she solemnly lay.

Netball was her passion
She had given it her all.
But until quite recently
Her skills had hit a brick wall.

She could n't quite explain it
And why she felt that way.
But something unfathomable
Had affected her outstanding play.

An incredible sting of worthlessness
Had settled in her mind.
A feeling of sheer failure
Of the worst and dreadful kind.

Today her team was selected
To play their match Inter-state.
She knew she had to do something
Before it was too late.

Lee could continue to sit there
And ponder over it all.
Or she could sort herself out
And support them after all.

Whatever she decided
Needed to be done a tad quick.
An opportunity like this
Disappears in a flick.

Excitement hopscotched through her
And engulfed her like a storm.
Propelling her forward
While powerful thoughts began to form.

A sudden pang of fear took hold
As Lee made her way to the door.
She raised her chin pugnaciously
And scampered across the floor.

An incredible feeling of self-worth
Started pumping through her veins.
Lee grabbed her thoughts together
And held on tightly to those reins.

With renewed strength and courage
She mustered up all her force.
She knew what had to be done
As she bolted out like a horse.

To the netball match she fled
Her spirit no longer abated.
She was riled up and fired up
All worries were instantly deflated.

Lee had determined within herself
To join them in their play.
And not one iota of doubt
Could spoil her peace this day.

She stepped boldly into the arena
And shuffled quickly through the crowd.
When her netball team spotted her
Their chants became deafeningly loud.

They raised their hands in joy
And jumped frantically in the air.
Their booming voices rippled through
Creating a delightfully ceremonious affair!

Lee had made a choice
A decisive one that day.
To share in the teams joys
And to support them, in every possible way.

8. Nature's Artwork

By Liesel Kippen 🩶

A carpeted mass covers the ground
Shapes varied, from oval to round.
Beautifully scattered and daintily clad
With auburn shades, shimmering just a tad.
A sprinkling of green and chocolate brown
Sits on the surface of the earth like a crown.
Streaks of light seep through the spaces
Covering all the dimly-lit places.

The foliage presents a picturesque sight
An artist's work, done in crimson light.
A pageant of colour is splashed all about
For a more breathtaking scene, you'd have to scout.
Rolled up and green, withered and frail
The foliage leaves a pungent, rustic, earthy trail.
A meandering path is vaguely seen
Where furry little creatures had recently been.

Burly trunks, ancestral and tall
Dominate acutely like a slanting wall.
Merged together, fortified at their base
Then extending outwards; a wish-bone interface.
Branches scrawny, protruding like a nose
Forked out menacingly in an undignified pose.
A spirited boulevard nestles overhead
While blotches of sunlight plague the soil a romantic red.

9. Fallen Oak

By **Liesel Kippen** 🩶

Day became night as an icy haze crept over the lake
The wind's howl echoed through the trees.
Distant sounds kept the occupant awake
They taunted and teased in the chilled evening breeze.

Somewhere, a drum beat continuously
As wood crackled around the fire's light.
A rumble of thunder murmured casually
The rain's steady pitter patter disrupted the still night.

A thunderous crash jolted the man to his feet
Then a shuffling of shoes scraped the pine floors.
The deserted dwelling now alive, though indiscreet
As a muffled voice filtered through the doors.

The ominous chiming of the grandfather clock
Sliced through the silence like a knife.
The man stood frozen, then clambered out in shock
As a jagged oak sprawled like an open wound, without life.

Its decayed remnant silhouetted the night scene
This languished, grotesque, charred, forest spleen.

10. The Lake District

By **Liesel Kippen**

Lake District ~ Windermere

A satiny mist descends over the Lake
Her profound beauty, breathtaking, no fake.
Silvery, cotton wool hangs over the land
Made infinitely by God's loving hand.

The shroud sits majestically on high
Reigning supremely in an opaque sky.
Faint, feathery, sleepy and white
Morning has broken after the dreary night.

Clouds nestle in nature's arms below
In the forested, myriads of trees that grow.
This beautifully fragrant forest air
Emits a scent so delicately rare.

Sweet and smoky, inebriating smells
A strong and earthy pungent dwells.
Delicately seductive and distinctly faint
These authentic odours acutely taint.

Enormous trees, fern-like and green
Autumn colours, even tangerine.
Grand and leafy titanic heights
All bask in the sun's raw golden lights.

Ancient, rugged, shaggy and tall
Orange trees, crimson and small.
Sustained images of beauty unfolds
As the subtle nuances of daybreak takes hold.

Flowering plants, alluringly adorned
With protective involucre, fleetingly scorned.
The height from the trees enlarges the view
While shadows and colours permeate on cue.

Well-kept lawns and neatly trimmed grass
Encapsulates a mass of filmy glass.
Its gauze-like features and liquid state
Creates a lake so elegantly ornate.

Chirping birds provide a musical interlude
Tweets so profound, they graciously soothe.
Unconstrained and unrehearsed
While Windermere's poets add these to their verse.

The rolling hills of the countryside
Are lavishly sprawled on landscapes, wide.
They subtly keep quiet profiles
As nature's grandeur stockpiles.

Imposing landforms, this scenic place
Displays her trinkets with modest grace.
England's District Lake, a literary treasure
Hides untold wealth of infinite measure.

11. God's Perfect Timing

By Liesel Kippen 🖤

All things happen in God's perfect time
A sometimes unfathomable paradigm.
He's never early and He's never late
But always on time, while you deliberate.

God handles matters in His own special way
He carefully ponders over what you have to say.
Trusting God is the way to go
It dispels the obstacles that bring you low.

Having faith is not an easy feat
It requires you to rise above defeat.
It urges you to focus on the light
As you challenge your darkest and blackest night.

Prayer helps to understand God's plan
A fact not easily grasped by man.
It provides insight and intellect galore
And equips you with strength, as you seek to explore.

God's timing is worth the wait
It eases your burdened, unsettled state.
It causes you to rise and boldly stand
As you lean upon His Almighty hand.

God's timing may seem a tad late
But God is instrumental in determining our fate.
He never rushes as He orchestrates
Every aspect of our lives He recreates.

As you pray meaningfully to God each day
He'll show you His faithful and perfect way.
A road that is filled with immeasurable peace
Diligently sought after, where stresses cease.

God makes everything beautiful in time
Blessings that last for an incredible lifetime.
All we are required to do is wait
For God's perfect timing to resonate and advocate.

12. Where is the love?

By **Liesel Kippen** 🤍

All this hatred
All this pain.
It seems this world
Has gone insane.
No brotherly love
No Christian care.
Not an ounce of affection
Anywhere.

Where is the love?
Where did it go?
Has it been tainted
By COVID's bitter blow?

No beauty in sight
No passionate embrace.
The world has begun
To target RACE.
No kindness around
No joy in the air.
Not a drop of compassion
Anywhere.

Where is the love?
Where did it go?
Has it been tainted
By COVID's bitter blow?

So much sadness
So much gloom.
The future looks bleak
With unending doom.
So much hurting
So much strife.
So much evil
Perforates life.

Where is the love?
Where did it go?
Has it been tainted
By COVID's bitter blow?

Endless misery
Endless harm.
Endless uncertainty
Not a modicum of calm.
Endless dying
Endless unrest.
Society deteriorates
At its toxic best.

Where is the love?
Where did it go?
Has it been tainted
By COVID's bitter blow?

Destroyed buildings
Destroyed stores.
All this insanity
Permeates our shores.
Destroyed history
Destroyed cultures.
This present era
Torn to shreds by vultures.

Where is the love?
Where did it go?
Has it been tainted
By COVID's bitter blow?

Endless pillaging
Endless looting.
Endless killing
Endless shooting.
Endless thieving
Endless fighting.
Endless anarchy
Callously inciting.

Where is the love?
Where did it go?
Has it been tainted
By COVID's bitter blow?

Unparalleled madness
Unparalleled uproar.
Antagonistic behaviour
Allowed to soar.
Unparalleled disorder
Unparalleled turmoil.
Rotting and festering
Nature's beautiful soil.

Where is the love?
Where did it go?
Has it been tainted
By COVID's bitter blow?

Let's end this bitterness
Let's end this fight.
Let's end this havoc
That lurks in sight.
Let's seek to build
Let's seek to grow.
Let's seek to harness
A reconciling afterglow.

For THERE dwells the love
Which won't ever go.
It WON'T become tainted
By COVID's bitter blow.

13. Positive Mindset Power!

By Liesel Kippen

We are shaped by our thoughts
That fill our heads each day.
They dominate our minds
And influence what we say.
They activate the mind's processes
Which act on our emotions.
A negative flow of these ideas
Could trigger inconceivable notions.

Positive thoughts are treasures
They bring healing to the soul.
They comfort a saddened heart
And fill up an untenanted hole.
They encourage bounty feelings
Of peace and joy to soar,
While tapping on love's affections
So intense, it comes to the fore.

They flood the body's senses
With excitement and intrigue.
They invigorate those weary limbs
Which have been drained by fatigue.
The mind is set in motion
Too powerful to impede.
These cognitive displays
Step in and brazenly stampede.

As you feed on positivity
And drink from its refreshing well,
It warms the embers of the heart
And philosophical concepts swell.
They conjure up an inner peace
Too dominant to erase,
While subtly removing
Disillusionment's phase.

They take on challenges with ease
Unlike some of us.
It soon becomes apparent
There's no need for all the fuss.
Warm emotions start to flow
As positive thoughts are deployed.
Successful ventures emerge
And, with oozing confidence, are convoyed.

A positive mindset is fulfilling
It adds richness to life,
By eliminating all the stresses
That cause infinite strife.
It enables one to adapt
To life's many challenging fronts,
While the mental and emotional state
Endure resiliently, without any grunts.

A positive mindset is like a flower
That takes its time to bloom.
All its artistic petals
Stand gloriously in the face of gloom.
They brilliantly and defiantly blossom
In the midst of winter's cold,
And if they lose a petal or two
In spring, they reappear, exceedingly bold.

14. Unrivalled Beauty (Shape Poem)

By Liesel Kippen 🩶

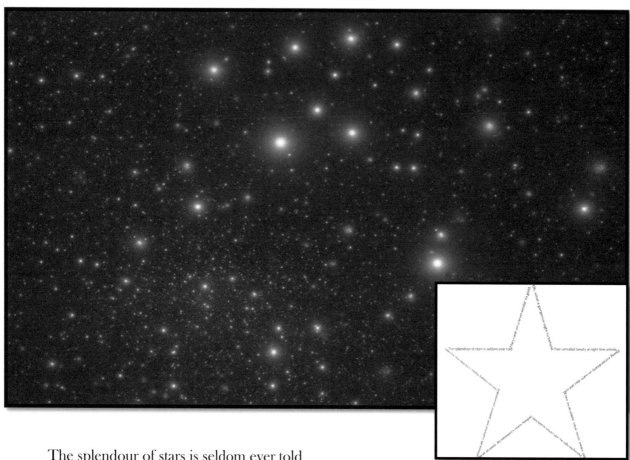

The splendour of stars is seldom ever told
They rank on a level similar to gold.
Oh, what a gorgeous sight to behold
Their unrivalled beauty at night time unfolds.
Shining extraordinarily on warm days and cold
Their incalculable value never wears old.
Piercing the night sky, with corners acutely bold
Majestic and stately, like Kilimanjaro's creamy Marigold.
Whimsically scattered with patterns uncontrolled
Their ever-changing displays, in the Milky Way, inscrolled.

15. Autumn Shades

By **Liesel Kippen** ♥

In the heart of an enchanting forest
Below the scarlet sky,
Lies a beautifully adorned cluster
Of woody trees nearby.
The view from above is picturesque
Nothing can quite compare,
Her beauty stretches far and wide
In fact, almost everywhere.

The blue wintry hazy grey
No longer enshrouds the place,
A subtle silvery puffed up mass
Provides an invisible case.
Autumn has tiptoed in
And leaves begin to fall,
Each, a different shade of red
They heed to fall's exuberant call.

Lofty trees gracefully adorn the scene
Transformed into beautiful shapes,
Lethargically, they raise their heads
As light settles demurely at their napes.
The rays from the sun modestly seep
Through their branches, in wisps of white,
Often intricately entangled
Between sinews coiled quite tight.

The forest has a magical feel
A satisfying ambience too,
The beautiful brown and orangey shades
Cascade and envelope the view.
Mellow rose, palest gold
Soft teal and pebble grey,
Oyster white, coral light
Aubergine and rose taupe.

The alluring stream meanders below
Sublimely rugged barks,
Somewhere in this grandeur
Sound melodious mimicries of larks.
Chattering noises soon emerge
And permeate the air,
While a series of high whistled notes
Are pitched from birds, quite rare.

The mystical intrigue that dominates
Has a therapeutic and breathtaking view,
It unfolds gradually in stages
Timed effortlessly and on cue.
While this beauty cannot be duplicated
Or replicated in any way,
A mirrored reflective symmetry
From its languid waters display.

Printed in the United States
By Bookmasters